THE TOXIN THAT CAME TO DINNER

DAVID SANDOVAL

ISBN 13: 978-0-9914700-4-4

Copyright © 2018 by David Sandoval and Panacea Community, LLC

All rights reserved. No part of this publication may be reproduced, distributed, or transmitted in any form or by any means, including photocopying, recording, or other electronic or mechanical methods, without the prior written permission of the publisher, except in the case of brief quotations embodied in critical reviews and certain other noncommercial uses permitted by copyright law. For permission requests, write to the publisher, addressed "Attention: Permissions Coordinator," at the address below.

Panacea Community, LLC
PO Box 29004
Santa Fe, NM 87592

www.ThePanaceaCommunity.com
(877) 335-2683

Ordering Information:
Quantity sales. Special discounts are available on quantity purchases by corporations, associations, and others. For details, contact the publisher at the address above.

Printed in the United States of America

TABLE OF CONTENTS

A Tribute to Albert Szent-Györgyi 1

The Human Detox Project..4

The Big Problem...8

You Would Think We Would Have Learned Something 20

The #1 Marker for Heart Disease and Autoimmune Disease..22

THE SECOND BRAIN 26

What is the GUT Microbiome and Why is it Important?........28

GUT FEELINGS 31

Happy Hormones...33

What Causes an Unhealthy Microbiome? 37

Glyphosate and Its Assault on the Microbiome........................40

Pets and Glyphosate..43

Warning Signs of a Potentially Disrupted Microbiome............46

Restoring and Rejuvenating Your Microbiome 49

LEARN MORE ABOUT BIOME MEDIC 57

TESTIMONIALS...58

ABOUT THE AUTHOR...62

Chapter 1
A Tribute to Albert Szent-Györgyi

I want to begin this book with a tribute to Albert Szent-Györgyi, because Albert Szent-Györgyi is one of the most important figures in history that you have never heard about, even though we study his work in our science classes in school, and benefit from many of his discoveries. I have no doubt that millions of lives have been saved by his groundbreaking work, and now, nearly 30 years after his death, this Nobel Prize winning laureate may be responsible for saving millions more.

Despite his being born in Hungary in the late 1800s, Albert had a storied academic career. He began his research career in Bratislava finally ending up at the University of Groningen where his work focused on the chemistry of cellular respiration. This work landed him a position as a fellow at Cambridge University north of London. He received his PhD in 1927 for work on isolating an organic acid, which he dubbed "hexuronic acid", from adrenal gland tissue. His scientific career took on additional importance with his groundbreaking study of the chemical changes that occur when cells utilize foodstuffs, such as carbohydrates, fats, and protein, a process sometimes known as biological combustion.

In the course of his studies, Szent-Györgyi isolated a molecule from adrenal glands that lost and regained hydrogen atoms. This "hydrogen carrier," contained six carbon atoms, and surprisingly had the properties of both a sugar and an acid. Szent-Györgyi christened it "hexuronic acid." In 1930 Szent-Györgyi and his research fellow Joseph Svirbely found that "hexuronic acid" was actually the unidentified antiscorbutic factor, now known as vitamin C.[1] At the University of Szeged, Szent-Györgyi conducted a landmark experiment on guinea pigs, which, like humans, must ingest foods containing vitamin C to maintain their health since it cannot be produced within their bodies. During these experiments, Szent-Györgyi proved that vitamin C enables the body to efficiently use carbohydrates, fats, and protein.[2] His ability to identify hexauronic acid as Vitamin C was among the foundations of modern nutrition. Ten years after receiving his PhD and four years after his discovery, Szent-Györgyi was awarded the Nobel Prize in

---

[1] Albert Szent-Györgyi - From Wikipedia the Free Encyclopedia April 4 2018 https://en.wikipedia.org/wiki/Albert_Szent-Gyorgyi

[2] American Chemical Society National Historic Chemical Landmarks. The Discovery of Vitamin C by Albert Szent-Györgyi 22 May 2018 http://www.acs.org/content/acs/en/education/whatischemistry/landmarks/szentgyorgyi.html

Physiology & Medicine.³ He further proved the connection between Vitamin C and the catalysis of fumaric acid. Due to this groundbreaking work, some could say he is the Father of the "vitamin" industry.

Szent-Györgyi went on to identify and study actin and myosin, proteins responsible for muscle contraction, and demonstrated that the compound adenosine triphosphate (ATP) is the immediate source of energy necessary for muscle contraction. He later identified flavonoids as vital to strengthening capillary blood vessels.

In 1933, Szent-Györgyi set about to find additional, natural sources of antiscorbic acid. "I took red peppers into the laboratory ... [and by] about midnight I knew that it was a treasure chest full of vitamin C." At the time of his discovery, tens of millions suffered from Vitamin C deficiency and over one million people per year died of scurvy, a disease caused by the deficiency of one single nutrient that's found in food!

He subsequently established The Foundation for Cancer Research. During his time there he isolated a fraction of wheat germ that dramatically increased gut health in animals by acting as powerful prebiotic and co-factor. He died, however, before a practical use for this discovery was identified. While it may not have gained notoriety during his lifetime, as you will see in the coming pages, it may be his most important discovery, and save millions more lives.

---

[3] "Albert Szent-Györgyi - Biographical". Nobelprize.org. Nobel Media AB 2014. Web. 21 May 2018. http://www.nobelprize.org/nobel_prizes/medicine/laureates/1937/szent-gyorgyi-bio.html

Chapter 2

The Human Detox Project

The dedication to Albert Szent-Györgyi is appropriate considering the important role he may play in solving one of modern man's greatest challenges - a challenge that will be illustrated in these pages. Before I begin to tell this story, I want to thank you for taking the time to read it and to educate yourself about what may be the single greatest threat to the health and prosperity of our world today.[4] In fact, it impacts millions of Americans' lives *right now* and millions more across the globe.

To what am I referring? Many scientists and respected researchers believe the proliferation of an agricultural chemical called glyphosate may be disrupting our ability to

---

[4] Widely Used Herbicide Linked to Cancer Daniel Cressey, Nature magazine on March 25, 2015 https://www.scientificamerican.com/article/widely-used-herbicide-linked-to-cancer/

thrive and even to survive as a species. The complications caused by widespread glyphosate toxicity could be in part responsible for a massive increase of physical, mental and immune challenges that are now pervasive among our children, ourselves and our parents. The common thread is the food we eat and the environment in which we live. Both of these are now sources of potentially lethal glyphosate contamination. The World Health Organization has declared that this chemical is a human health hazard and as of July 7, 2017, against Monsanto's unsuccessful challenge in court, the state of California EPA has declared that glyphosate is a carcinogen and causes cancer.[5]

Now, because of all of this evidence, the city of Los Angeles has recently voted to ban the use of Roundup, a.k.a. glyphosate, within 100 feet of children's play areas, dog parks and recreation centers.[6]

On the following pages, I am going to illustrate both the seriousness as well as the prevalence of this problem, and while raising awareness and education are vital, we are also going to focus on solutions. We desperately need solutions to detoxify our bodies and rebuild our health that may have been damaged through our exposure to this newly-identified chemical that you may have never even heard about (until now).

---

[5] California EPA Becomes First U.S. Agency to Declare That Roundup Causes Cancer Nathan Donley March 28, 2017 https://www.biologicaldiversity.org/news/press_releases/2017/glyphosate-03-28-2017.php

[6] Los Angeles Restricts Use of Monsanto's Roundup in Public Areas The Sustainable Pulse Oct 27 2017 https://sustainablepulse.com/2017/10/27/los-angeles-restricts-use-of-monsantos-roundup-in-public-areas/#.WwRY5Mgh1TZ

I believe that ultimately, glyphosate will be added to a list of banned chemicals, *like so many others before it that were once approved and deemed to be safe for use in and around our homes and were later proven to cause cancer, mental disorders & birth defects.*

The previous use of asbestos in home insulation led to a huge rise in mesothelioma, a rare type of lung disease. Lead found in paint is associated with learning disabilities, birth defects and damage to lungs and kidneys. DDT in agriculture literally caused stillbirths and the extinction of species. These are just a few examples of how our home environment has become toxic, despite our faith in government and industry to protect us.

In foods, many preservatives, sweeteners and food colorings were originally labeled safe and later found to drastically affect our health or even cause cancer.

Think: red, blue, and yellow dyes (cancer), high fructose corn syrup (diabetes), Monosodium Glutamate/MSG (obesity), aspartame (cancer), rGBH (Mad Cow Disease), even the irradiation of food that's since been banned. Now, we once again find ourselves confronting a new danger and facing a significant new threat to our health. The threat comes from the incredible proliferation of this agricultural herbicide in homes, on the highways, and now in community parks, a chemical that was originally created to support GMO farming practices.

Having it on farms is dangerous but avoidable, unfortunately, over the years its use has extended far beyond the fields. Even if you choose to eat organic or non-GMO verified food as a way of avoiding this toxic agricultural chemical, you can still be exposed to potentially dangerous levels without even knowing it!

Even foods that are labeled non-GMO could now have high levels of toxic residues found in them. The toxin of which we speak, glyphosate, is the primary chemical in Roundup, which is the main herbicide that is used in genetically modified farming. According to a study done by the US Geological Survey, glyphosate was detected in our water - 86% in rain alone! Ditches and drains measured 71%, soil 63%, and even 18% in large rivers![7]

---

[7] Glyphosate and AMPA in U.S. streams, groundwater, precipitation and soils - Journal of the American Water Resources Association 2014 https://pubs.er.usgs.gov/publication/70046159

Chapter 3
The Big Problem

Today, there is evidence that just as these herbicides are able to kill all of the weeds and all of the non-genetically modified organisms that grow in soil, they also have been shown to kill the living organisms that grow and live within your human microbiome, or your gut (AKA your "second brain"). And that is the root of a huge host of problems![8]

> The human microbiome, or microbiota, is a collection of all the microscopic organisms such as bacteria that reside in our tissues; including our skin, mouth, lungs and digestive tract. We have an immensely symbiotic relationship with these microbiota. A majority of these microorganisms inhabit our gut, and for the intents and purposes of this book, the gut microbiome may be referred to solely as the microbiome.

---

[8] Weed-Whacking Herbicide Proves Deadly to Human Cells By Crystal Gammon, Environmental Health News on June 23, 2009 https://www.scientificamerican.com/article/weed-whacking-herbicide-p/

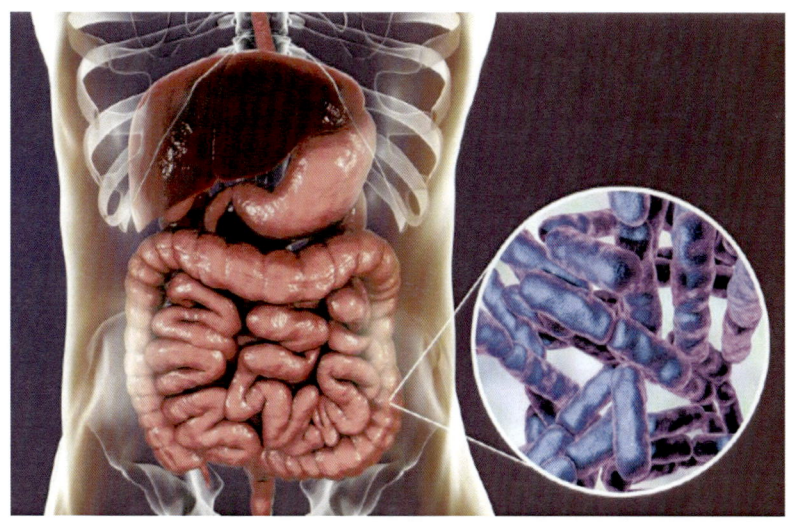

According to timeline charts created by the Journal of Organic Systems study, there's a direct and alarming correlation, over the past 20 years, between the rise of use of glyphosate and major disease rise in the USA. The most direct correlations between the increased use of glyphosate on crops and the increased incidence of health issues are as follows: bile duct cancer, kidney and renal pelvis cancer, urinary/bladder cancer, thyroid cancer, deaths due to hypertension, deaths due to stroke, deaths due to obesity, diabetes, disorders of lipoprotein metabolism, renal disease deaths, inflammatory bowel disease (Crohn's, and ulcerative colitis), deaths due to intestinal infection, autism, senile dementia, deaths due to Alzheimer's, and deaths due to Parkinson's disease.[9]

---

[9] Genetically engineered crops, glyphosate and the deterioration of health in the United States of America Journal of Organic Systems, 9(2), 2014
http://www.organic-systems.org/journal/92/
JOS_Volume-9_Number-2_Nov_2014-Swanson-et-al.pdf

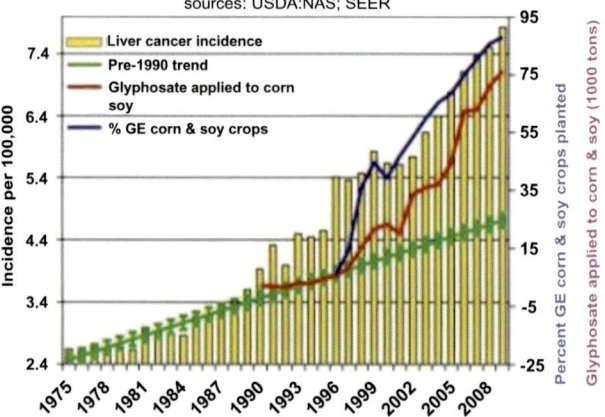

Figure 7. Correlation between age-adjusted liver cancer incidence and glyphosate applications and percentage of US corn and soy crops that are GE.

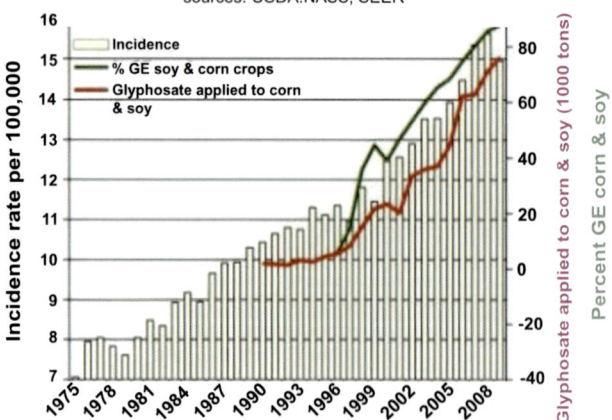

Figure 8. Correlation between age-adjusted kidney cancer incidence and glyphosate applications and percentage of US corn and soy crops that are GE.

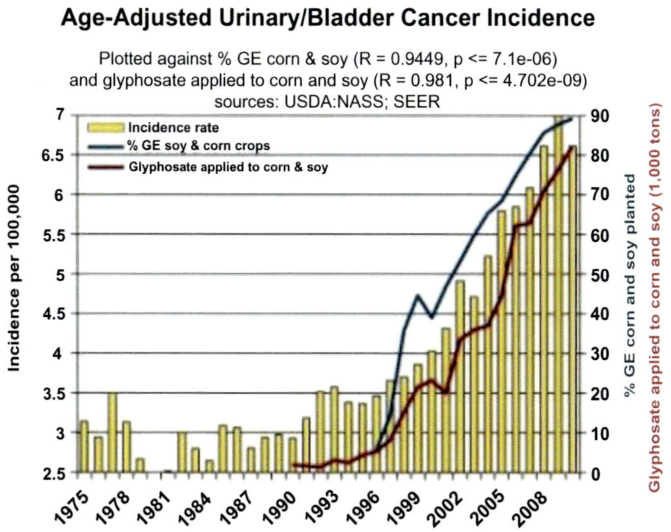

Age-Adjusted Urinary/Bladder Cancer Incidence

Plotted against % GE corn & soy (R = 0.9449, p <= 7.1e-06)
and glyphosate applied to corn and soy (R = 0.981, p <= 4.702e-09)
sources: USDA:NASS; SEER

Figure 9. Correlation between age-adjusted bladder/urinary tract cancer and glyphosate applications and percentage of US corn and soy crops that are GE.

Thyroid Cancer Incidence Rate (age-adjusted)

Plotted against glyphosate applied to U.S. corn & soy (R = 0.988, p <= 7.612e-09)
along with %GE corn & soy crops R = 0.9377, p <= 2.152e-05
sources: USDA:NASS; SEER

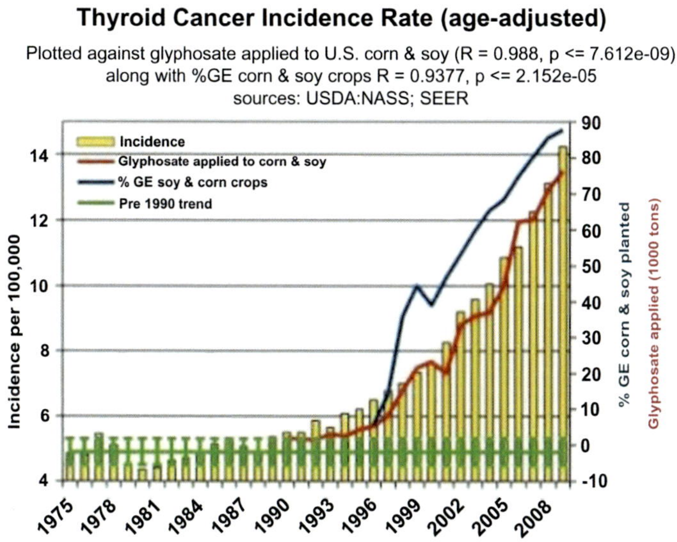

Figure 10. Correlation between age-adjusted thyroid cancer incidence and glyphosate applications and percentage of US corn and soy crops that are GE.

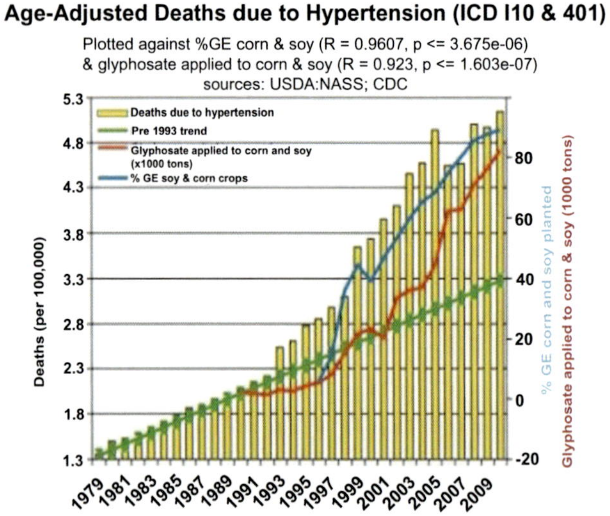

Age-Adjusted Deaths due to Hypertension (ICD I10 & 401)

Plotted against %GE corn & soy (R = 0.9607, p <= 3.675e-06)
& glyphosate applied to corn & soy (R = 0.923, p <= 1.603e-07)
sources: USDA:NASS; CDC

Figure 10. Correlation between age-adjusted thyroid cancer incidence and glyphosate applications and percentage of US corn and soy crops that are GE.

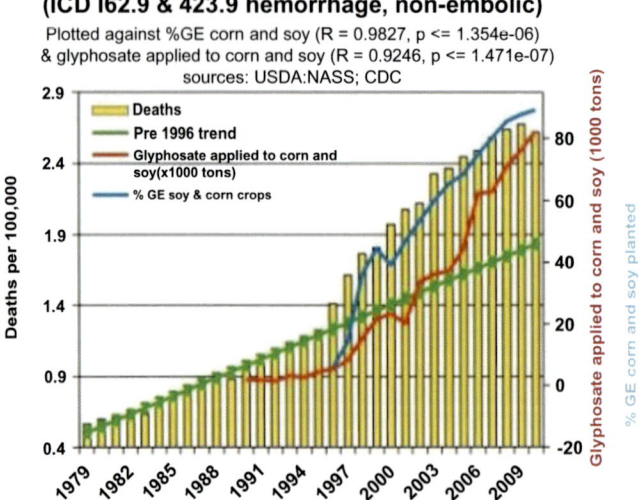

Age-Adjusted Deaths due to Stroke
(ICD I62.9 & 423.9 hemorrhage, non-embolic)

Plotted against %GE corn and soy (R = 0.9827, p <= 1.354e-06)
& glyphosate applied to corn and soy (R = 0.9246, p <= 1.471e-07)
sources: USDA:NASS; CDC

Figure 12. Correlation between age-adjusted hemorrhagic stroke deaths and glyphosate applications and percentage of US corn and soy crops that are GE.

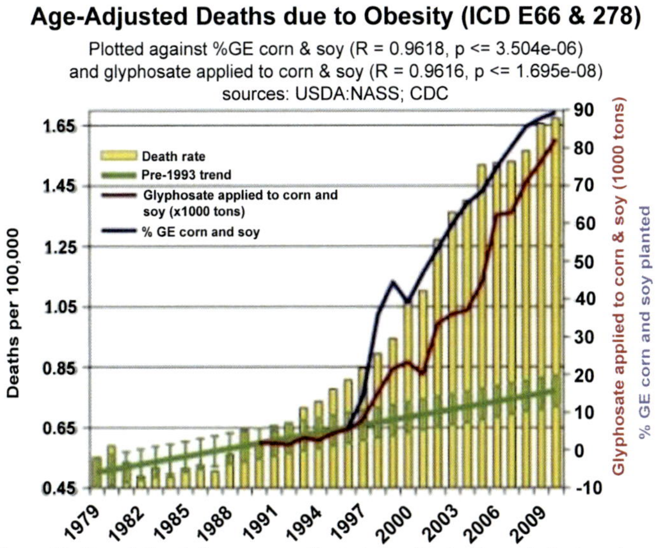

Age-Adjusted Deaths due to Obesity (ICD E66 & 278)

Plotted against %GE corn & soy (R = 0.9618, p <= 3.504e-06) and glyphosate applied to corn & soy (R = 0.9616, p <= 1.695e-08)
sources: USDA:NASS; CDC

Figure 13. Correlation between age-adjusted obesity deaths and glyphosate applications and percentage of US corn and soy crops that are GE.

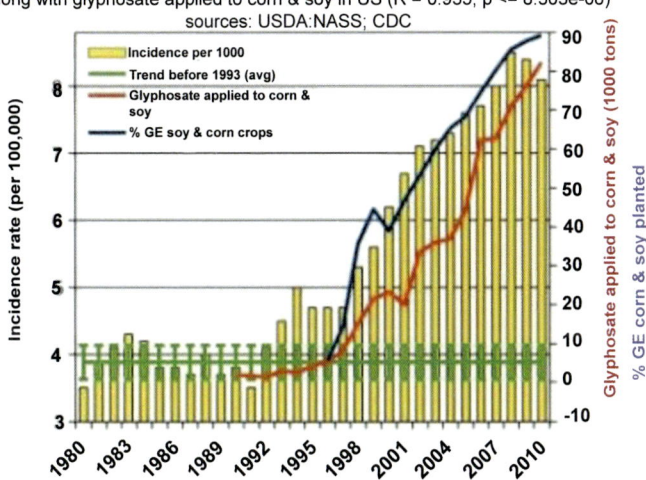

Figure 14. Correlation between age-adjusted diabetes incidence and glyphosate applications and percentage of US corn and soy crops that are GE.

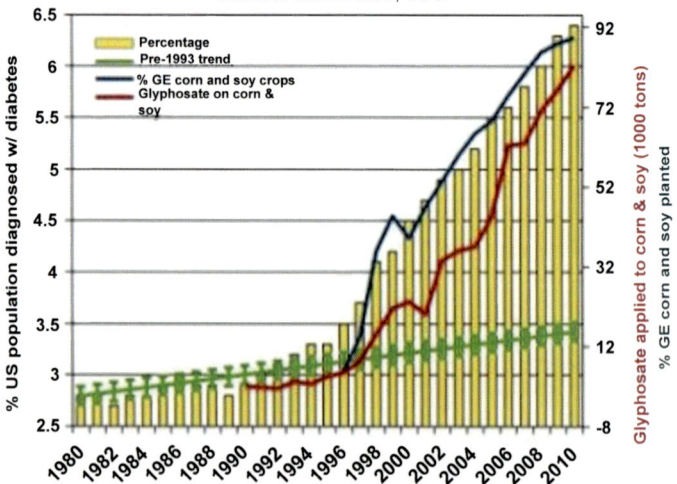

Figure 15. Correlation between age-adjusted diabetes prevalence and glyphosate applications and percentage of US corn and soy crops that are GE.

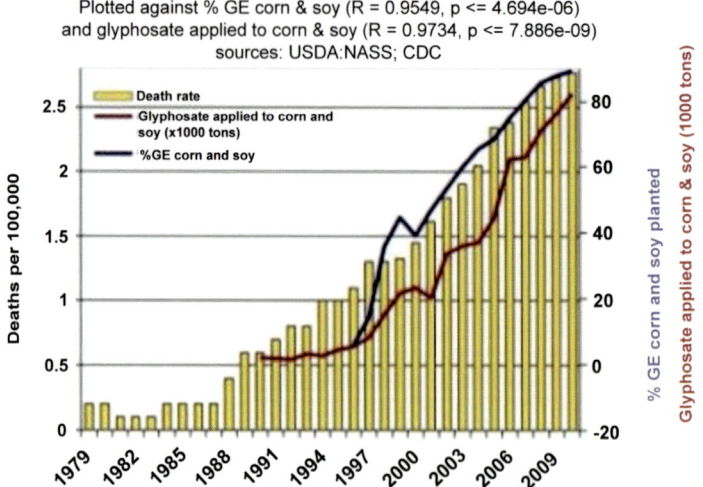

Figure 16. Correlation between age-adjusted lipoprotein disorder deaths and glyphosate applications and percentage of US corn and soy crops that are GE.

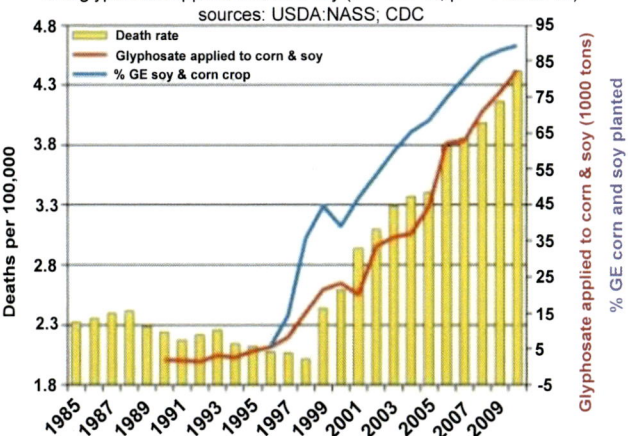

Figure 18. Correlation between age-adjusted End Stage Renal Disease and glyphosate applications and percentage of US corn and soy crops that are GE.

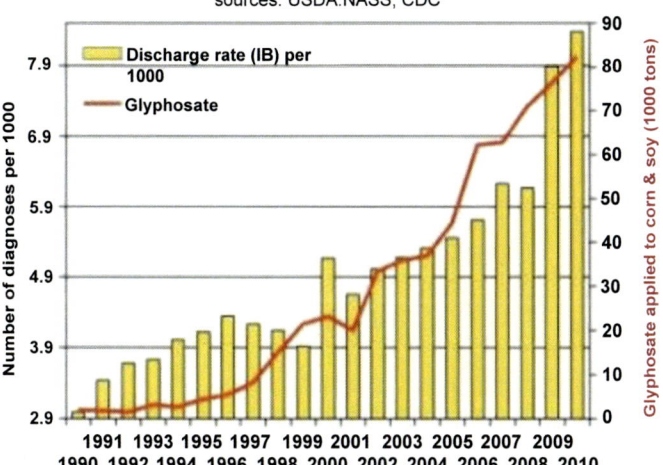

Figure 20. Correlation between inflammatory bowel disease and glyphosate applications to US corn and soy crops.

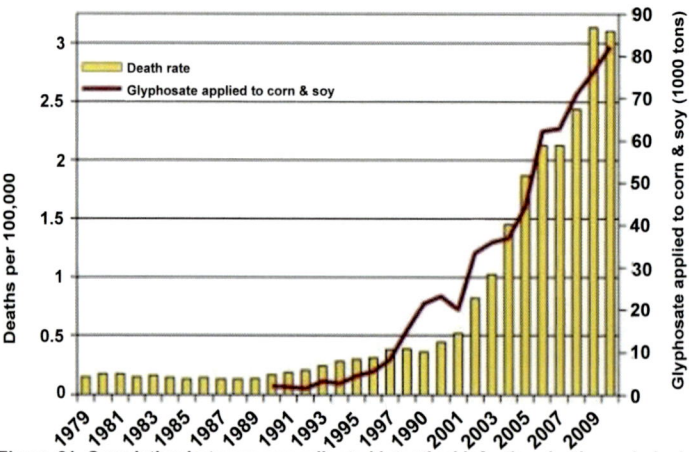

Figure 21. Correlation between age-adjusted intestinal infection deaths and glyphosate applications to US corn and soy crops.

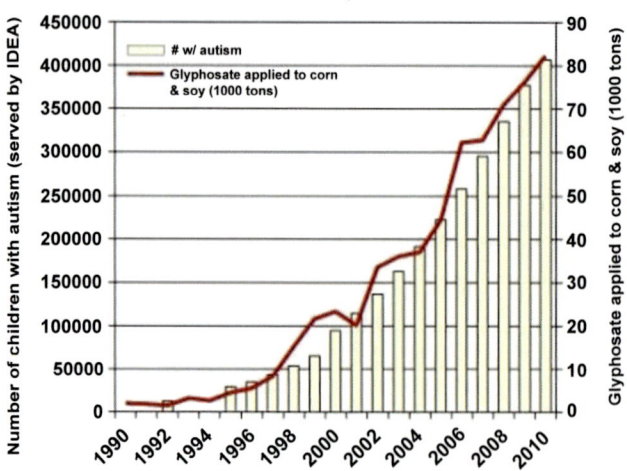

Figure 23. Correlation between children with autism and glyphosate applications.

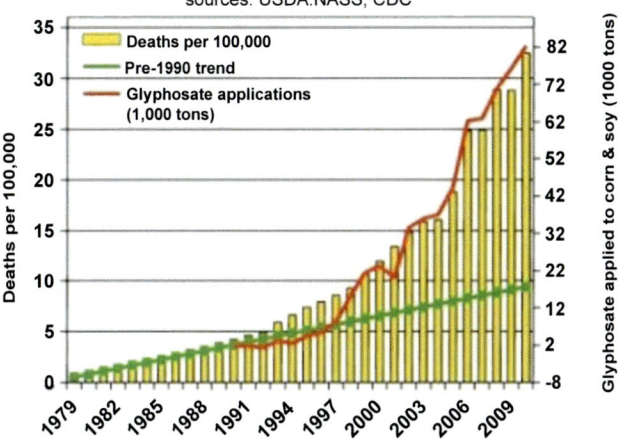

Figure 24. Correlation between age-adjusted dementia deaths and glyphosate applications.

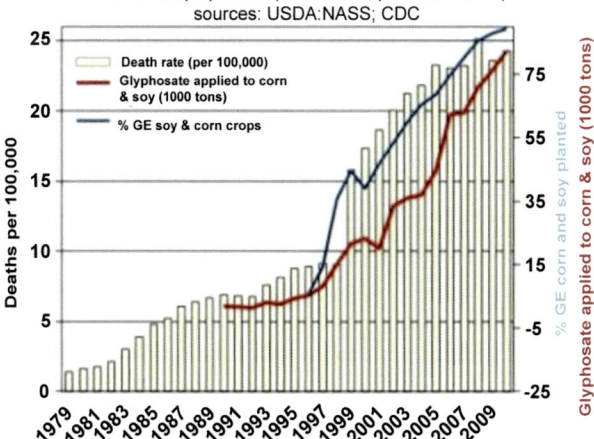

Figure 25. Correlation between age-adjusted Alzheimer's disease deaths and glyphosate applications and percentage of US corn and soy crops that are GE.

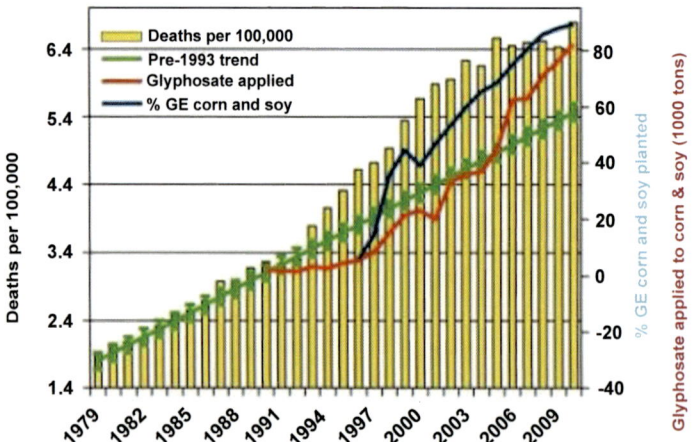

Figure 26. Correlation between age-adjusted Parkinson's disease deaths and glyphosate applications and percentage of US corn and soy crops that are GE.

According to the authors of the study, "a huge increase in the incidence and prevalence of chronic diseases has been reported in the United States (US) over the last 20 years. Similar increases have been seen globally. The herbicide glyphosate was introduced in 1974 and its use is accelerating with the advent of herbicide-tolerant genetically engineered (GE) crops. Evidence is mounting that glyphosate interferes with many metabolic processes in plants and animals and glyphosate residues have been detected in both. Glyphosate disrupts the endocrine system and the balance of gut bacteria, it damages DNA and is a driver of mutations that lead to cancer."

The increased use of glyphosate has led directly to the increase of health issues in Americans in almost a one-to-one correlation. And so, here's the issue: we have microorganisms in our gut, which are delicate and have a really important job, but they may be being killed by glyphosate.

Genetically modified organisms are the only ones that will not be killed by the glyphosate. Glyphosate is designed to kill organisms that are not genetically modified. I repeat, glyphosate is designed to kill organisms that are not genetically modified.

"Glyphosate, patented as an antimicrobial by Monsanto, has been shown to disrupt gut bacteria in animals, preferentially killing beneficial forms and causing an overgrowth of pathogens. Two other properties of glyphosate also negatively impact human health – chelation of minerals such as iron and cobalt, and interference with cytochrome P450 (CYP) enzymes, which play many important roles in the body."[10]

When we eat food with the residue of glyphosate in it, it can destroy the mucosal layer of critical organisms including bacteria that protect the villi. And so, the destruction of the organisms leads to the destruction of the villi and the combination of organisms and villi are what we call the microbiome. To put it simply, when we eat food that is covered in glyphosate, then that glyphosate goes into our gut, it can kill our organisms and cause a whole host of issues. That's the bottom line. The glyphosate may be killing our microbiome and causing massive health issues that otherwise could be avoided.

---

[10] Glyphosate, pathways to modern diseases II: Celiac sprue and gluten intolerance Anthony Samsel1 and Stephanie Seneff Dec. 2013 https://www.ncbi.nlm.nih.gov/pmc/articles/PMC3945755/

Chapter 4
You Would Think We Would Have Learned Something

Rachel Carson, the author of Silent Spring, is my inspiration. She raised her voice and proved that the actions of highly-motivated individuals can overcome the greed of multinational corporations. She called attention to the fact that an agricultural chemical was causing irreparable damage to humans and to our planet. After her work, I had hoped that this tragedy would never happen again. Unfortunately, 56 years later, we are faced with a nearly identical crisis. And it is ironic how her words, spoken 56 years ago, ring just as true today.

To paraphrase Rachel Carson's words, once again it is the time for highly-motivated individuals to take a stand! Because "for the first time in the history of the world, every human being is now subjected to contact with dangerous chemicals from the moment of conception until death…

These chemicals are now stored in the bodies of the vast majority of human beings, regardless of age. They occur in the mother's milk, and probably in the tissues of the unborn child." —Rachel Carson, *Silent Spring*

Though Rachel Carson was speaking about the unknown dangers of DDT, the same can be said of glyphosate. And just like DDT before it, very little research has been presented to prove its safety, and significant research has been indicated to prove its dangers.

Yet glyphosate, the active ingredient in Monsanto's Roundup, is the most heavily used chemical weed killer in human history, as a result of the widespread adoption of genetically engineered crops - now grown on more than 175 million acres in the United States and more than 440 million acres around the globe. Additonally, the weight in pounds of glyphosate used on crops in the U.S. has risen from 7,683,070 in 1990, all the way to 249,906,307 by 2014.[11]

New scientific evidence shows that probable harm to human health could begin at ultra-low levels of glyphosate e.g. 0.1 parts per billions (ppb), while popular foods tested for glyphosate measured between 289.47 ppb and at levels as high as 1,125.3 ppb.[12]

---

[11] Trends in glyphosate herbicide use in the United States and globally Environmental Sciences Europe Charles M. Benbrook 2 February 2016 https://doi.org/10.1186/s12302-016-0070-0

[12] Glyphosate: Unsafe on Any by Plate - Food Democracy Now! by David Murphy Henry Rowlands https://s3.amazonaws.com/media.fooddemocracynow.org/images/FDN_Glyphosate_FoodTesting_Report_p2016.pdf

Chapter 5

The #1 Marker for Heart Disease and Autoimmune Disease

Now that we have established that the presence of high glyphosate levels in the body is cause for concern, let us turn our attention to a substance called C-Reactive Protein, which is known to be the #1 biomarker for heart disease and autoimmune disease. Unlike glyphosate, it is known to every doctor in the United States and tested by every credible lab.

C-Reactive Protein (CRP) is produced by the liver, and it is able to reduce inflammation by identifying the virus, pathogen, or even a dead and dying cell that is contributing to the inflammation. The CRP will then mark these organisms as targets for our immune system to eliminate from the body. Our white blood cells, t-cells, killer cells, and macrophages create an army that responds to this C-reactive protein defense system.[13]

Unfortunately, when there is excess inflammation, there will also be excess CRP and the CRP can begin to mark cells that are not ready for elimination and that are not a threat to the body. When this happens, we refer to it as an "autoimmune response", AKA an "autoimmune disease."

From a clinical point of view, a CRP level equal to 1mg per liter of blood is considered within a safe range. As the CRP climbs to 3 milligrams, you have technically entered the zone where the CRP levels are considered dangerously high. At this level, the instance of cardiovascular diseases begin to increase (the average heart attack victim has allowed their CRP level to exceed 10mg/ liter). This is a highly measurable and predictable result of rising CRP level.

According to the American Heart Association Journals, "....approximately 25% of the US population has levels of CRP greater than 3 mg/L, the cut point for high risk."[14]

That means that most middle aged Americans are suffering from higher levels of CRP than is considered safe and millions more are suffering from dangerously high levels of CRP.

As noted earlier, most people who suffer from heart attack or stroke have a high C-Reactive Protein average. If you can get your CRP down to below 1 mg per liter, your

---

[13] C-reactive protein 6-4-2018 https://medlineplus.gov/ency/article/003356.htm

[14] C-Reactive Protein A Simple Test to Help Predict Risk of Heart Attack and Stroke September 23, 2003, Volume 108 Iss. 12 http://circ.ahajournals.org/content/108/12/e81

chances of heart attacks, strokes, and autoimmune diseases can be decreased exponentially.

This is important because we're going to illustrate to you a safe and effective method to dramatically reduce your CRP levels (an average of 75%) in as little as six weeks by helping to repair your gut microbiome, also known as your second brain.

It is recommended that every American know their CRP levels, and the preferred method is to take two separate tests two weeks apart and take the average of the two numbers. However, a single test is often times a great indicator of your CRP level. You can ask your doctor to include this in your next blood panel, and they will definitely comply. If not, you need a new doctor.

Typically a medical doctor will recommend chelation therapy to reduce CRP levels. Though according to the first large scale chelation therapy clinical trial sponsored by NCCIH and the National Heart, Lung, and Blood Institute, infusions of EDTA chelation therapy produced a modest reduction in cardiovascular in those without diabetes, and a larger benefit for those who have diabetes. They found that chelation therapy plus adding in high-dose vitamins and minerals created the greatest reduction in risk of cardiovascular events versus a placebo. During this study, 16% of people receiving chelation stopped the trial due to adverse reactions with 4 people having serious complications and 2 of them died during the trial.[15]

According to Stephanie Watson, the Executive Editor of Harvard Women's Health Watch, published on Harvard

---

[15] Chelation for Coronary Heart Disease 9-24-17 https://nccih.nih.gov/health/chelation

Health Publishing of Harvard Medical School, "each treatment costs $75 to $125, and people often undergo dozens of these three-hour-long infusions over a period of several months. All in all, a treatment course can exceed $5,000—and it isn't typically covered by health insurance. That would be money well spent if it truly prevented heart attacks and strokes. But neither TACT nor prior studies suggest that's the case."[16]

This Process requires multiple doctor's visits, appointments, and payments, which is a huge inconvenience for a relatively low return, in comparison to the solution we will be sharing with you later in this book.

---

[16] Chelation therapy offers small, if any, benefit for heart disease Stephanie Watson 3-26-13 https://www.health.harvard.edu/blog/chelation-therapy-offers-small-if-any-benefit-for-heart-disease-201303266030

Chapter 6
THE SECOND BRAIN

One of the many dangers of glyphosate exposure is its effect on our "brains". Yes, plural- as in, more than one. It has been said that the gut microbiome is the second brain of the body sending out more neurotransmitters from the gut than the brain located in our head.

According to Dr. János Simon, MD, Chief Surgeon at the Department of Internal Medicine, Clinical Hematologist and Dietitian, the human GI tract which houses the microbiome is vital to over 70% of our immunity and digestion. Today, leading authorities and researchers believe there may be over 20 conditions that may be tied to a compromised microbiome. The restoration of the microbiome could possibly be the answer to many nagging health issues plaguing our society today. This is truly a mega-crisis.

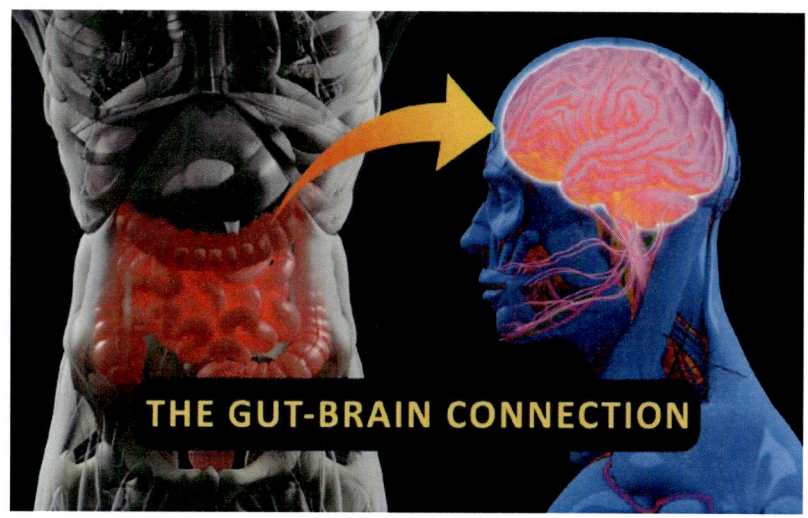

THE GUT-BRAIN CONNECTION

Though just like every human health crisis that we have faced before, we have gone in search of an effective solution, and as has happened with each of these crises before, a solution may have been found. However, without recognizing the problem, the solution is useless.

Chapter 7
What is the GUT Microbiome and Why is it Important?

The human microbiome is the most important part of the body that you've probably never heard about. When we hear things like, "I had a gut feeling," or "go with your gut," it may actually be true. Modern scientists have called the microbiome the "second brain" because it sends out neurotransmissions similar to how the brain does. Dr. Michael Gershon, MD, Professor of Pathology and Cell Biology and Author of The Second Brain states, "technically known as the enteric nervous system, the second brain consists of sheaths of neurons embedded in the walls of the long tube of our gut, or alimentary canal, which measures about nine meters end to end from the esophagus to the anus. The second brain contains some 100 million neurons, more than in either the spinal cord or the peripheral nervous system."

The microbiome is the last stop in your body in the digestive process. The microbiome is in the lowest part of your intestines and although it is at the end of the line it is actually the most critical part of activating the gut's intelligence because all of the waste and nutrients from the food you eat end up in your colon, including both the beneficial and dangerous things. In fact, the reason why your immune system is triggered by the microbiome is because that is where disease beings (in the gut). Strengthening the microbiota strengthens the entire body-- weakening it does the opposite!

Your microbiome has the intelligence to figure out what to keep and what to eliminate. It will do its best to filter out the toxins and only allow vital nutrients to pass through the villi into the bloodstream. One symptom of a "sick" microbiome is that this sortation process is compromised and the body will reabsorb toxins while eliminating important vitamins and minerals. This is often referred to as "leaky gut syndrome" and as I keep noting, the negative effects of a

"Inside our bellies, we have an extensive intestinal lining covering more than 4,000 square feet of surface area. When working properly, it forms a tight barrier that controls what gets absorbed into the bloodstream. An unhealthy gut lining (AKA Leaky Gut) may have large cracks or holes, allowing partially digested food, toxins, and bugs to penetrate the tissues beneath it. This may trigger inflammation and changes in the gut flora (normal bacteria) that could lead to problems within the digestive tract and beyond." [17] ~Marcelo Campos, MD

---

[17] Leaky gut: What is it, and what does it mean for you? Marcelo Campos, MD September 22, 2017 https://www.health.harvard.edu/blog/leaky-gut-what-is-it-and-what-does-it-mean-for-you-2017092212451

destroyed microbiome may be far reaching and devastating to the health of our children, ourselves and our parents.

According to Dr. Leo Galland, director of the Foundation for Integrated Medicine, the following symptoms might be signs of leaky gut:

- Chronic diarrhea, constipation, gas or bloating
- Nutritional deficiencies
- Poor immune system
- Headaches, brain fog, memory loss
- Excessive fatigue
- Skin rashes and problems such as acne, eczema or rosacea
- Cravings for sugar or carbs
- Arthritis or joint pain
- Depression, anxiety, ADD, ADHD
- Autoimmune diseases such as rheumatoid arthritis, lupus, celiac disease or Crohn's

Chapter 8
GUT FEELINGS

According to Justin Sonnenburg and Erica Sonnenburg, PhDs, "the gut microbiota influences the body's level of the potent neurotransmitter serotonin, which regulates feelings of happiness. Some of the most prescribed drugs in the U.S. for treating anxiety and depression, like Prozac, Zoloft, and Paxil, work by modulating levels of serotonin. And serotonin is likely just one of numerous biochemical messengers dictating our mood and behavior that the microbiota impacts."[18]

According to Dr. Gershon, serotonin produced from the second brain could play a part in autism.

---

[18] Gut Feelings–the "Second Brain" in Our Gastrointestinal Systems [Excerpt], Justin Sonnenburg, Erica Sonnenburg, Scientific American 2015 https://www.scientificamerican.com/article/gut-feelings-the-second-brain-in-our-gastrointestinal-systems-excerpt/

Gershon has discovered that the same genes involved in synapse formation between neurons in the brain are involved in the alimentary synapse formation. "If these genes are affected in autism," he says, "it could explain why so many kids with autism have GI motor abnormalities" in addition to elevated levels of gut-produced serotonin in their blood. So the system of passing signals is broken- and so is the neural development of our children.

FACTS ABOUT AUTISM[19]

- "Autism is the fastest-growing developmental disability."
- "About 1 percent of the world population has autism spectrum disorder."
- "Prevalence in the U.S. is estimated at 1 in 59 births."
- "More than 3.5 million Americans live with an autism spectrum disorder."
- "Prevalence of autism in U.S. children increased by 119.4 percent from 2000 (1 in 150) to 2010 (1 in 68)."
- "Prevalence has increased by 6-15 percent each year from 2002 to 2010."
- "Autism services cost U.S. citizens $236-262 billion annually."
- "Cost of lifelong care can be reduced by 2/3 with early diagnosis and intervention."
- "The U.S. cost of autism over the lifespan is about $2.4 million for a person with an intellectual disability, or $1.4 million for a person without intellectual disability."
- "35 percent of young adults (ages 19-23) with autism have not had a job or received postgraduate education after leaving high school."

---

[19] Facts and Statistics Autism Society 2015 http://www.autism-society.org/what-is/facts-and-statistics/

Chapter 9
Happy Hormones

Hormones regulate many of our body's most important systems and biorhythms, and many key hormones actually begin in our gut. One of those is serotonin, which is the building block for melatonin, and melatonin is the "deep sleep hormone", which helps our body to reduce stress and activate our immunity.

When you're sleeping really well, all of your body's systems are activated at a higher level. The relationship between the gut releasing serotonin, which gets converted to N-acetyl serotonin (and then to melatonin), is directly correlated to better immune function and overall health. This is an incredible symbiotic relationship between the gut and our sleep pattern.

"People who have problems with sleep are at increased risk for developing emotional disorders, depression, and anxiety."
~Dr . Lawrence J. Epstein

THE EFFECTS OF SLEEP AND MOOD

- Sleep and mood are interconnected; a lack of sleep can cause irritability and stress, while healthy sleep can improve overall well-being.
- Chronic Insomnia can lead to anxiety or depression.
- Some studies show that even partial sleep deprivation can have a profound effect on mood.

The microbiome is a field of fine hairs called the villi, covered by a light coating of microorganisms called a mucous membrane. Imagine a green grassy field with bubbles floating all along the top and those bubbles are the bacteria and the green grass are the villi. The majority of nutrients absorbed in the body occur via the villi, which is located within the small intestine, an essential part of the microbiome.

Another essential part of the microbiome are the bacteria, which play many roles, including stimulating the immune system, preventing growth of pathogenic bacteria, synthesizing vitamins and hormones that assist with the storage of fats, and eliminating toxins. In fact, the microbiome is involved in the majority of toxin elimination.

If toxins are not eliminated via urine, sweating, breathing or defecating, they could reenter the body and create autointoxication, meaning toxins aren't eliminated from the body and they re-enter into the bloodstream. Autointoxication can happen when you don't have proper functioning of the microbiome due to Leaky Gut as we discussed earlier.

Another key piece to understanding the gut microbiome is to know that when the second brain is healthy, the big brain stays healthy as well.

According to multiple publications in PubMed, there is shocking evidence that an unhealthy microbiome could be a direct cause of neurodegenerative diseases.[20]

"While the enteric nervous system does not seem capable of thought as we know it, it does communicate back and forth with our big brain—with profound results." Says Jay Pasricha, M.D., director of the Johns Hopkins Center for Neurogastroenterology. This leads experts to believe that an unhealthy gut could be a direct tie to Alzheimer's, Parkinson's, and Dementia.

Studies such as these show promise and indicate further research is warranted. It also indicates that immediate dietary modification may be recommended for those who cannot wait for the results of such studies to be irrefutably confirmed.

"Gut microbiota can modulate host brain function and behavior via microbiota-gut-brain axis, including cognitive behavior. Your diet, use of antibiotics, alcohol consumption, and regularity can all induce alterations of gut microbiota and gut physiology and also host cognitive behavior, increasing or decreasing risks of Alzheimer's."[21]

In other words, your second brain is vitally important to your mental functioning. Bad gut, bad brain! The

---

[20] Human gut microbiota: the links with dementia development PMCID: PMC5291774 2016 Nov https://www.ncbi.nlm.nih.gov/pmc/articles/PMC5291774/

[21] The second brain and Parkinson's disease PubMed - Eur J Neurosci. 2009 Sep;30(5):735-41. doi: 10.1111/j.1460-9568.2009.06873.x. Epub 2009 Aug 27.

increased permeability of our intestine and blood-brain barrier induced by gut microbiota disturbance will increase the incidence of neurodegeneration disorders.

Promising studies such as this one indicate further research is warranted in this topic and addressing the health of the microbiome may be appropriate.

NEURODEGENERATIVE DISEASES

In terms of human suffering and economic costs, neurodegenerative diseases are among the top diseases in terms of human suffering and economic costs.

The Alzheimer's Association estimates that by 2050 11 million to 16 million Americans will have Alzherimers, with a new case appearing every 33 seconds.

Alzheimer's Disease International estimates that there were 46.8 million people worldwide living with dementia in 2015 and this number will reach 131.5 million in 2050.[22]

As many as one million Americans and 10 million people worldwide live with Parkinson's disease.

The cost of Parkinson's, including treatment, social security payments and lost income from inability to work, is nearly $25 billion per year in the United States alone.[23]

---

[22] World Alzheimer Report 2016 - Alzheimer's Disease International https://www.alz.co.uk/research/WorldAlzheimerReport2016.pdf

[23] Statistics on Parkinson's Disease - Parkinsons Association of the Carolinas May 2018 https://www.parkinsonassociation.org/facts-about-parkinsons-disease/

Chapter 10

What Causes an Unhealthy Microbiome?

During a clinical trial in the UK and Sweden, researchers gave participants one of four commonly prescribed antibiotics or a placebo. They checked on participants' oral and gut microbiomes right after the week of antibiotics, and one, two, four, and 12 months afterward.

The effects varied depending on which antibiotic the person took, but generally, while the oral microbiome bounced back quickly, some of the bacteria in the intestines suffered a disturbingly negative outcome. The report concluded that, "depending on the type of antibiotics, the effects of a single antibiotic exposure on the human gut microbiome can be very aggravating and prolonged. Additionally, based on metagenome predictions and the affected taxa, we can conclude that a single use of antibiotic treatment… in a healthy population may severely affect short-chain fatty acid (SCFA) production in the gut. Undesired effects of clindamycin consist of gastrointestinal disturbances, the incidence varying between 2% and 20%. Although members of the current study population did not present with any clinically significant side effects, exposure to antibiotics had a significant effect on the gut ecosystem." "Clearly," the study reads, <u>"even a single antibiotic treatment in healthy individuals contributes to the risk of resistance development and leads to long-lasting detrimental shifts in the gut microbiome."</u>[24]

Resistance development refers to the adaptive changes bacteria undergo to withstand attempts to kill them, such as antibiotic use in medication and in livestock and poultry production. Antibiotics and other drugs that are used to prevent or cure serious bacterial infections become less effective and may not work at all since the bacteria have become resistant to them.

In fact, superbugs resistant to all antibiotics are now a serious threat around the world. That is the reason why people have begun to rethink the use of antibiotics. Many health experts have realized over the years that the use of antibiotics would kill many of the beneficial organisms inside the body. It is also known that this can happen to those who drink alcohol. Alcoholism or consuming a high amount of alcohol in a short time (binge drinking) can also kill off colonies of healthy microorganisms, and I want to note that this totally offsets other purported "benefits" of regular

---

[24] Same Exposure but Two Radically Different Responses to Antibiotics: Resilience of the Salivary Microbiome versus Long-Term Microbial Shifts in Feces http://mbio.asm.org/content/6/6/e01693-15.full.pdf

alcohol use. Another issue that can disrupt the microflora in your gut is constipation. Not having enough fiber is a problem, because fibers not only assist in pushing and cleansing, they are also critical sources of prebiotics for friendly bacteria. For this reason, fiber is far more important than you may have realized, and may even be as important or more important than probiotics. As you know, in the past, a simple solution might be to take some fiber, take some probiotics and maybe even change our eating and our drinking habits. With these simple changes, the microbiome would typically return in full health.

Chapter 11

Glyphosate and Its Assault on the Microbiome

However, there's a new assault on the microbiome that's affecting millions of people in a way that is so devastating, they may never recover.

As you may know, there is a growing movement toward fighting genetically modified organisms (GMO's). More and more people want their food to be labeled so they can identify and avoid genetically modified food. The reason why is because there is a fear that eating genetically modified food has serious and unknown consequences. But what if we have been focusing on the wrong thing the entire time? I'm not saying there isn't a problem with genetically modified food - I'm convinced there is. What I am saying is that the clear and present danger is not the genetically modified food itself, but instead as stated earlier, it seems that the problem is the chemical glyphosate, a key ingredient in a weedkiller known as Roundup. But even if you eat non-GMO food, it does not mean it is glyphosate-free. Just because the seeds are not genetically modified does not mean that they have not used Roundup as a desiccant as they do in wheat and grain crops.

Sarah, the "Healthy Home Economist" states that, "pre-harvest application of the herbicide Roundup or other herbicides containing the deadly active ingredient glyphosate to wheat and barley as a desiccant was begun as early as 1980. It has since become routine and over the past 15 years has been used as a drying agent 7-10 days before harvest within the conventional farming community",[25] a.k.a. traditional crops.

According to Dr. Stephanie Seneff of MIT, desiccating non-organic wheat crops with glyphosate before a harvest was promoted by chemical companies in the 1990's. This practice is now contaminating most of the non-organic wheat in the United States with glyphosate. Seneff explains that when you expose wheat to a toxic chemical like glyphosate, it releases more seeds resulting in a greater yield: "It 'goes to seed' as it dies. At its last gasp, it releases the seed," says Dr. Seneff.

Glyphosate is also being used on your highways, on your schoolyard, in your apartment building, your condo, in your parks, everywhere. Since glyphosate is absorbed into the plant's cellular structure in order to kill weeds or unwanted plants, the chemical is unable to be removed from GMO crops and other plants by traditional methods of washing,

---

[25] The Real Reason Wheat is Toxic (it's not the gluten) Aug 24 2017 http://www.thehealthyhomeeconomist.com/real-reason-for-toxic-wheat-its-not-gluten/

peeling, baking or brewing. In more recent years, a growing number of studies have found glyphosate in common foods, human urine, breast milk, beer, and even 85% of tampons.[26]

Dr. Seneff has also found that "Glyphosate disrupts the shikimate pathway, an essential biological pathway in plants and many microbes. It is argued that glyphosate is nearly nontoxic to humans because human cells don't possess this pathway. However, our gut microbes use this pathway to produce the aromatic amino acids which they supply to the host. These are essential building blocks of proteins and precursors to a long list of important biologically active molecules, such as the neurotransmitters serotonin, melatonin, dopamine and epinephrine, thyroid hormone, melatonin, and the B vitamin folic acid. As discussed above, just a deficiency in serotonin alone can cause a host of health and mood problems."[27]

---

[26] Glyphosate: Unsafe on Any Plate – Food testing results and scientific reasons for concern. Report by Food Democracy Now! And the Detox Project

[27] Glyphosate's Suppression of Cytochrome P450 Enzymes and Amino Acid Biosynthesis by the Gut Microbiome: Pathways to Modern Diseases. Anthony Samsel and Stephanie Seneff. Entropy 2013; 15: 1416-1463.

Chapter 12
Pets and Glyphosate

As we examine the danger and the threat to humans due to the proliferation of glyphosate in our food and the environment, we must also begin to look at its impact on the health of man's best friend: our pets. The cats and dogs that live in our environment with us will oftentimes be eating pet food that contain high levels of glyphosate, as well as table scraps that we might feed them, thus exposing them to human food that may have a glyphosate contamination. Many commercial dog foods in particular contain grains, seeds and legumes, which are all highly likely to contain glyphosate.

Additionally, since pets do not wear shoes like humans, when they walk in the grass on people's lawns, parks and fields, their paw pads are more likely to absorb chemical fertilizers, herbicides and pesticides in the grass such as Disulfoton, Dicamba, and glyphosate.

Because of all these points, an animal's total exposure may be much, much greater than a human's. There is mounting evidence that this is a problem that needs to be addressed.

I was lucky enough to hear a dissertation by a woman named Alex, who actually spoke to a number of veterinarians and specialists on the subject and some of the information that was shared was rather disturbing. Each of the veterinary practitioners reported a dramatic increase in the rate of conditions, maladies and illnesses among cats and dogs, much more so than had been seen in the past.

Below are some of the most compelling statements, quotes and data that might make you think twice about where you walk your dog, where you let them play, the food you feed them, and the food that you share, as well as its quality of life and the number of years that you'll be able to enjoy its' company, not to mention the medical bills and heartache that might ensue considering your pet's widespread exposure to a chemical like glyphosate.

Quotes from the video *"Protect Our Pets from GMOs and Pesticides"* created by The Institute for Responsible Technology (https://youtu.be/w5hvB43kNzU):

Jeffrey Smith - "The primary toxin in Roundup is called glyphosate. The World Health Organization has classified glyphosate as a probable human carcinogen. But they also said for animals, it's not probable, it does cause cancer."

Dr. Marlene Siegal, DVM - "We need to make changes. We need to think differently, we need to change our belief systems, and we need to create the consumer demand for the very foods that will enable our pets to live the longest, healthiest life possible. And until we make that line in the sand, it's not going to happen."

Dr. Michael W. Fox - "I see the creation of GMOs, genetic engineering, biotechnology, as the last step for the human species to tamper with the earth's regulatory and creative processes. It's the invasion on the sanctity of life, purely for human profit."

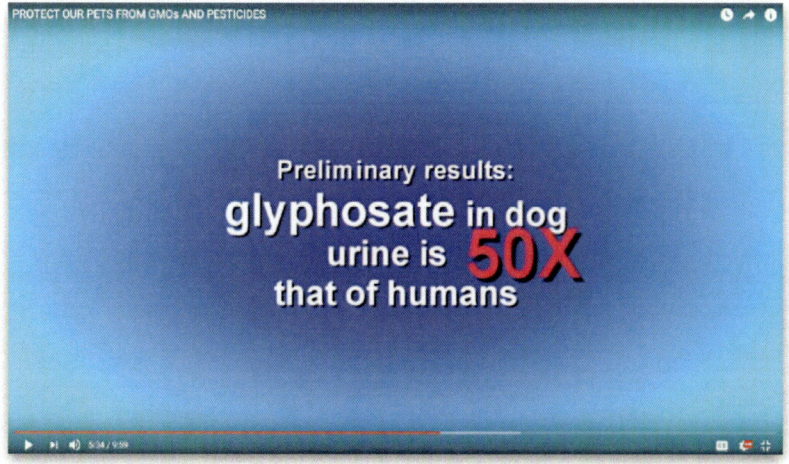

Chapter 13

Warning Signs of a Potentially Disrupted Microbiome

Even just a small disruption to the microbiome could lead you to feel sluggish, tired, give you headaches, body aches, poor elimination, poor digestion, gastrointestinal distress and ultimately what is called 'leaky gut' or gut permeability.

Once the gut becomes more permeable, you have autointoxication, which is waste from your body that cannot leave your body. The waste re-enters your body, which causes a whole host of problems. The microbiome is so delicate that even if you damage 10% of it, you are seriously compromising your overall health. In today's world, you could be destroying 25%- 50% of your microbiome without knowing it, and I see people suffering massive health issues and they don't seem to know why. They can't figure out what's causing the symptoms because the symptoms of gut permeability strongly mimic symptoms of very serious diseases. However, upon testing by doctors you often find that you don't have a serious disease, and the doctors don't know what to do other than prescribe more medications and antibiotics which further destroy your microbiome.

According to Dr. János Simon MD, Chief Surgeon at the Department of Internal Medicine, Clinical Hematologist and Dietitian, here are some of the signs when intestinal bacterial balance is out of control:

- Gas and bloating
- Constipation and/or diarrhea
- Acid reflux
- Skin problems
- Overall sickness
- Headaches
- Urinary tract infections
- Trouble sleeping
- An inability to lose weight
- Sugar cravings, especially for heavily refined carbohydrates

"The ideal healthy ratio of 'good' to 'bad' bacteria is 85% to 15%, or 9 to 1. Unfortunately, due to lifestyle and environmental factors, the vast majority of the population is severely lacking when it comes to good bacteria, throwing their gut flora ratio completely out of whack," Dr. Simon says.

So, it's important that we begin to search out and educate ourselves of how to shut down gut permeability naturally, and we must learn to restore the integrity to the microbiome quickly and effectively. Unfortunately, we've gotten to a point in our society where a lot of the health issues a majority of people are feeling on a day-to-day basis have become accepted as the "norm." Most people don't realize what good health feels like because they haven't felt it in many years. But the good news is that you can experience good health and have the opportunity to prevent and even reverse many of the underlying causes of these devastating symptoms.

So now that we understand the problem, we need to start identifying solutions. In the following pages, we are going to show you how you can restore, revitalize, and re-energize your gut microbiome, the "second brain" that is so vital to your body's overall health.

"The ideal healthy ratio of 'good' to 'bad' bacteria is 85% to 15%, or 9 to 1."

Chapter 14

Restoring and Rejuvenating Your Microbiome

After identifying such a horrific threat to human health, we realized that it could be years, if not decades, before this chemical might be eliminated from our food and our environment, and faced with the reality that it is literally unavoidable, we have turned our attention to healing. We have turned our attention to repairing the damage done to our gut microbiome by using a novel combination of unique phytochemicals and food extracts. In nature, blocking damage is the first level of defense. It is preferred to suppressing because it prevents damage from ever occurring. Suppressing is nature's second option. It is preferred to repairing because the more you can suppress the damage, the less that needs to be repaired. So in nature, repairing is always the last resort. And so of course at first we tried to stop the use of this chemical, and we continue to fight that fight. And we not only encourage people to eat the purest organic food, but we seek to give them access to it as well. However, with our government's failure to block the use of this toxic chemical and with our ability to avoid and suppress it becoming more and more difficult, our current need is to repair. And with statistics reported in the Journal of the American Medical Association (JAMA)[28], we now see that many humans and most residents of the State of California are shown to have levels as much as 500% higher than is considered toxic by many experts.

And so in order to repair your gut health and ultimately your body's health, you must first effectively reduce or eliminate the cause of the damage. We must eliminate the reason why the damage is being done, in this case eliminate the glyphosate from our body. To accomplish this, you will need to first separate the glyphosate from the tissue, a.k.a. to free it so that it can be rapidly bound and eliminated in our excrement. This process of modulating the toxins, of binding the toxins, eliminating the toxins, of rebuilding the bacteria/mucosal layer, and ultimately re-growing the villi so they will be longer and stronger was our goal.

We sought to accomplish it by combining four powerful ingredients, each with its own unique purpose and place. To modulate the toxin, we chose fulvic acid. Fulvic acid is known by scientists to move minerals from the soil into the roots of plants, and to move these same electrolytes from plants into the bodies of the person or animal who might be eating that plant for nourishment. Fulvic acid is found in nature through the process of organic plant matter

---

[28] Excretion of the Herbicide Glyphosate in Older Adults Between 1993 and 2016 Paul J. Mills, PhD1; Izabela Kania-Korwel, PhD2; John Fagan, PhD2; et al Oct. 2017 https://jamanetwork.com/journals/jama/fullarticle/2658306

decompinsation releasing millions of beneficial healthy bacteria. According to Dr. Axe, "Fulvic acid and other humic acids contain a plethora of nutrients that improve gut health, including: trace minerals, electrolytes, fatty acids, silica, prebiotics and probiotics. These help nourish the digestive tract and also boost the ability of "good bacteria" to repopulate and form a healthy "microbiome" environment. We need a strong digestive system to build immunity, help control hormone production, regulate our appetite, reduce our stress response and much more."[29]

Secondly, once chemicals are being freed from the tissue, they will be bound by lactobacillus bacteria via an ingredient called LactoSpore®. Lactobacillus bacteria are an important friendly bacteria that bind toxins and prevent them from returning into the bloodstream, allowing our body to eliminate them through our excrement. Additionally, the spore effect will stimulate the production of colonies to protect the villi and rebuild the strength of the mucosal layer.

LactoSpore® is a probiotic preparation containing L(+) lactic acid producing microbial preparation from *Bacillus coagulans*. Several health benefits are known to be associated with probiotics consumption, including immune-boosting, protection against diarrheal diseases, nosocomial and respiratory tract infections, cholesterol lowering effects, attenuation of overt immune-inflammatory disorders and anti-cancer activities.[30]

---

[29] 7 Fulvic Acid Benefits & Uses: Improve Gut, Skin & Brain Health Dr. Axe May 2018 https://draxe.com/fulvic-acid/

[30] Bacillus coagulans MTCC 5856 supplementation in the management of diarrhea predominant Irritable Bowel Syndrome: A double blind randomized placebo controlled pilot clinical study Nutr J. 2016;15:21. doi: 10.1186/s12937-016-0140-6 http://www.lactospore.com/research/clinical

We also have found that the mineral depletion and mineral deficiencies created by the binding effect of glyphosate must be addressed in order to support the growth of both friendly colonies and villi, and all chemical reactions at the cellular level. This is accomplished by infusing the cocktail of ingredients with humic ore, which contains the widest variety of bioavailable elements and trace mineral complexes available on Earth.

Now the stage is set for perhaps the most impressive ingredient of all. At the beginning of this booklet, we spoke of vitamin C and its ability to reverse a common disease known as scurvy. Before the discovery of this vital nutrient and its food sources, billions of people suffered and millions died. The discovery of vitamin C in peppers, citrus, green vegetables, and potatoes launched what we know today as the vitamin or nutrition industry. A little-known fact is that the famous Hungarian doctor, Albert Szent-Györgyi, who discovered vitamin C and published the most profound research about it, rejected the substitution of ascorbic acid as vitamin C.

And today we know that ascorbic acid could never cure scurvy, and was in fact one of the greatest frauds ever perpetrated through supposed nutritional science. The compelling story here is that in order to fully repair the gut microbiome, we needed to reach back in history to an ingredient that was actually created by none other than Albert Szent-Györgyi himself, who believed it could ultimately be used as a treatment for cancer – which is fermented wheat germ extract.

So naturally, the next ingredient we used is the prebiotic known as PrebioSure – Digestive Wheat Germ Extract (DWGE). According to Dr. Csicsor, chemical engineer and member of the International Humic Substance Society, "protecting and nourishing existing bacteria is key to maintaining GI health - While we focus on supplementing our digestive system with different strains of probiotics from the outside it is important to nourish and protect our existing bacteria with nutrient rich nourishment. PrebioSure is an advanced and highly effective prebiotic containing biologically active compounds such as benzoquinone and a rich amino-acid profile. Thanks to the proprietary enzymatic extraction technology, PrebioSure is free of gluten, gliadin and fructans. The synergistic effect of the composition may be credited for nourishing the intestinal flora and enabling the repair and regrowth of the micro-villi in the mucosa, maintain its uniform and optimal absorption surface, resulting in healthy strong immune response to fight off pathogens. Human case and clinical study results – We tested DWGE with athletes and hospital patients suffering from IBS, Crohn's, Ulcerative Colitis, bloating, diarrhea and constipation. Every patient in the study experienced positive results and symptoms improved over the 30 day trial."

In addition to using LactoSpore, DWGE, and Fulvic Acid, we also included Humic Acid. Dr. Scicsor writes that "Humic substances are the biological-chemical-geological decomposition products of the living plant origin matter on Earth. Humus (soil-peat-coal) is the most relevant composition product of living matter. This decomposition process is also referred to as 'humification' and the main substances are Humic and Fulvic Acid. These well-defined chemical structure molecules are also categorized as organic-complex-forming molecules and are the intermediate product of decay of the living matter. This humification process happens over millions of years and can be defined as Pre-, Peak-, and Over-Humification stages."

Dr. Scicsor confirms that FulvicSure and HumicSure:
- Enter the cell membrane and effectively bond and inactive free radicals.
- Bond and inactivate toxins such as medicine and antibiotic residues, pesticide residues, Teflon, as well as inorganic toxic heavy metals such as aluminum, mercury, lead, and radioactive elements.
- Stimulate enzyme activity and transform nutrients into energy and biochemical building molecules.
- Supply the body with more than 70 biologically active organo-mineral complex micronutrients.

So, when you take these prebiotics and the humic ore and you mix them together, it becomes a very strong fertilizer to allow the bacteria to grow. While you're waiting for those bacteria to grow, you're infusing Lactospore, which is the lactobacillus spore, so that when it hits the gut, it explodes and grabs on to the toxins, helping to eliminate the toxins from the body. You're going to be rebuilding the original bacteria, while introducing other friendly bacteria in the Lactospore. You're going to be feeding the prebiotics and then you add the fulvic acid, which is going to help with the chelation of toxins, pesticides such as glyphosate and heavy metals.

While we're chelating the toxins out, we're allowing our natural environment for more healthy and indigenous bacteria to grow back. At this point we should be able to see the restoration of the microbiome in effect.

Like a highly-trained specialized task force, each of the 4 ingredients in Biome Medic each play a unique role to carry out the mission. The mission is to repair the gut microbiome and the way we do it is critical to our success.

The fulvic acid and the Lactospore work to free the toxin and to eliminate it. The minerals and the chicory root feed the friendly, indigenous bacteria and help them to regrow, and the patented DWGE helps strengthen and rebuild the villi.

In a double blind pilot study conducted on all of these ingredients combined in Purium's Biome Medic, the researchers found a reduction of glyphosate by 74% and a decrease in C-reactive protein by 75%.[31] According to Dr. Andrew Weil, M.D., "C-reactive protein (CRP) is a substance produced by the liver that increases in the presence of inflammation in the body. An elevated C-reactive protein level is identified with blood tests and is considered a non-specific marker for disease. It can signal flare-ups of inflammatory diseases such as rheumatoid arthritis, lupus, and vasculitis. Data from a large number of studies also suggest that over time, chronic low-level internal inflammation can lead to many serious, age-related diseases including heart disease, some forms of cancer, and

---

[31] The effects of a novel pre and probiotic in supporting improved gut health and lowering environmental toxin levels: a pilot study. Matthew C. Popkin, M.D. and James M. Blum, Ph.D. November 16, 2017

neurodegenerative conditions such as Alzheimer's and Parkinson's disease."[32]

In addition to Purium's flagship product, Biome Medic, indicating a large decrease in the levels of glyphosate and C-reactive protein in the subjects in the study, it was also awarded the prestigious Gold Seal by the Detox Project as a glyphosate detox solution.

My main focus as an educator and formulator over the past few decades has been, and will continue to be, bringing promising solutions to everyone seeking better health and more vitality in their lives. While we are at a critical time in history where disease is on the rise due to chemicals and toxins like glyphosate, we also have solutions at our fingertips to prevent, heal and reverse these debilitating diseases. I urge you to take action today by grasping hold of your destiny and taking control of your health. An entire movement can be created simply by one person taking action and sharing their results with others. I believe *you* are that person and together we can take control of our health and share this valuable information with the people we love the most.

Yours in health,
David Sandoval

---

[32] Elevated C-reactive Protein (CRP) Reviewed by Benjamin S. Gonzalez, M.D., May, 2016. https://www.drweil.com/health-wellness/body-mind-spirit/heart/elevated-c-reactive-protein-crp/

LEARN MORE ABOUT **BIOME MEDIC** AND JOIN THE MOVEMENT TODAY

Protect your gut from GMOs with this exclusive and proprietary formula of all-natural ingredients. This product can help flush harmful toxins, support "good" bacteria and repair your microbiome.

Awarded Gold Seal by the Detox Project as a glyphosate detox solution

Double-blind trial showed decrease in glyphosate by 74%

Double-blind trial showed decrease in C-reactive protein by 75%

TESTIMONIALS

Healed my gut & body

Gail Shouvlin on Jun 16, 2018

Biome Medic cleansed me of toxins & poisons. It helped heal my gut and body. In using Biome Medic in the 10 day cleanse, I no longer have hot flashes and for the 1st time ever I don't have spring allergies.

Changing Attitudes Toward Food

Alexandra Cornell on Jun 29, 2018

My son has been labeled as a super taster and a picky eater. However, the problem has been much greater and much more distressing than a cute label. We have had years of him not eating at all. He went from the 90th percentile to the 3rd one year, and after visiting 6 different doctors no one could tell us why. My daughter was breast fed only, but the hospital and doctors told me that my son needed additional nutrition when he was a baby and strongly urged me to add formula. As a somewhat older mom I thought I better; although this became what I think was the biggest culprit. My son had developed what I now know to be problems with his gut from all of the terrible ingredients in the formula. We even bought the health food kind often. When my daughter was born I would pump and feed him the extra I had often but I think the gut flora needed a lot of help to heal. As I had mentioned he didn't eat for years, only milk and once a day a cracker or two. It was terrifying. After having qigong performed on him he developed an appetite which was a miracle to see him eat and say "I am hungry!" but he had a long way to go. A dear friend suggested Biome Medic and it has been such a blessing! Now he is hungry and eats three meals and snacks. I believe this is healing the gut from all the GMOs in the formula. Thank you Purium. We will continue with our amped up qigong practice and biome medic on a daily basis.

My villi are alive and kicking once again!
Leslie Milthorpe on Jun 16, 2018

What are villi? It's those tiny micro, hair-like structures in your gut that helps to break down the food you eat so your body can absorb the nutrients from it. The more I learned what this was doing for me, the more I was intrigued to stay the course. What is the point in taking any sort of supplementation or "special diet" program if you can't absorb it. What I found for me, was my energy came back to life. I noticed things like my nails were stronger, my skin more clear and less digestive upset. One of the things I learned is that glyphosate prevents the absorption of minerals, so the outward changes I was seeing made sense as I chelated the glyphosate with continual regimen of Biome Medic. This is something I'm sticking with.

Bye bye belly trouble
Alica Grimwood on Jun 16, 2018

Have been taking Biome Medic for over a month now. I have noticed that my belly bloat has gone away and that I have fewer tummy and intestinal issues now than I was experiencing prior to adding this product to my daily regimen.

Great Product!
Adam on Jun 16, 2018

This product has helped me out so much! My gut health has improved so much and as a result has helped my bodies inflammation! Truly makes your whole body feel great!

Wisco Review
Karlie on Jun 15, 2018

I can finally breath, I am so free from my anxiety! Not to mention, I can enjoy wheat, and drink delicious craft beers again!

Life Changing
Mandi Rose on Jun 15, 2018

I was leary to start this product because I have celiac and it says on the bottle "contains gluten" however I learned that it has less gluten in the entire bottle than in 1 serving of gluten free pasta! So I had to give it a try. Since taking this, all my food sensitivities have improved and I can even enjoy ice cream again (in moderation of course). My gut feels happier than ever with noticeably less inflammation. Thank you Purium.

Truly amazing product
Jacqueline Rolfe on Jun 15, 2018
What an amazing product that you have. I've been taking this for 2 months and can already feel the difference; especially in the morning!!! And just the thought of it eliminating the Glyphosate from my body helps me feel even better. Thank you for getting this product to the market it is so very needed!!!

New skin - new me!
Kelly on Jun 15, 2018
After taking this for a few weeks, not only my skin begin to glow (and no, not pregnant! ha!), but my belly no longer hurt. Before Biome Medic, if I accidentally ingested wheat, it felt as though I'd swallowed a knife... not any more! Belly bloat is gone and my skin looks incredible.

Hello energy and focus, goodbye bloat!!
Sonia Magruder on Jun 14, 2018
I take this product religiously and never go a day without it. First, I love know that it's removing toxic glyphosate from my body and helping to support optimal gut health. Unfortunately no matter how good I eat, I know that there is still exposure to this chemical. As far as the results that I can feel, I rarely get bloated anymore, I have more mental focus and have tons of energy. Peace of mind, a calm digestive system and flatter belly are huge wins for me!

ABOUT THE AUTHOR

Purium's Co-founder and Visionary, Dave Sandoval, has made it his life's mission to change the world for the better. From nutrition and the environment to domestic violence and poverty, Dave has advocated on behalf of many causes. He's invited people into his home to personally help them get healthy, lose weight or achieve their goals. And, through his mentorship program, he has inspired all kinds of people, including celebrities, to get out into the world and make a difference. Dave founded Purium in post-riot Long Beach with Gandhi's philosophy, *"Be the change you wish to see in the world."*